D1860588

CASHMERE

CASHMERE

Three Weeks in a Houseboat.

A. PETROCOKINO

GYAN

Published by

GYAN

Gyan Publishing House
5, Ansari Road
Daryaganj, New Delhi-110002
Phone: 011-47034999, 9811692060
E-mail: books@gyanbooks.com

Distribution Network
gyanbooks.com
India, USA, Canada, UK, Australia, France

© Publisher

All rights reserved. No part of this work may be reproduced, stored, adapted, or transmitted in any form or by any means, electronic, mechanical, photocopying, micro-filming, recording or otherwise, or translated in any language, without the prior written permission of the copyright owner and the publisher.

ISBN: 978-81-212-9426-3 (PB)
First Published, 1920

2nd Impression 2023

Printed at: Gyan Press, Delhi.

The book is sold subject to the condition that it shall not, by way of trade or otherwise, be lent, resold, hired out, or otherwise circulated without the prior publisher's written consent.

CASHMERE

AUTHOR: A. PETROCOKINO

CASHMERE

Three Weeks in a Houseboat.

PLATE I.

My Dunga—Entrance.

Frontispiece

CASHMERE

Three Weeks in a Houseboat.

BY

A. PETROCOKINO

F.R.G.S.

With Twenty-five Plates.

LONGMANS, GREEN AND CO.

39 PATERNOSTER ROW, LONDON

FOURTH AVENUE AND 30TH STREET, NEW YORK

BOMBAY, CALCUTTA AND MADRAS

1920.

This little book does not pretend in any way to be a guide to Cashmere, but just what its name implies, and a tribute to it for the very pleasant, if hurried, time I spent there; and if anyone, who like myself had no time to spare in finding out when at Srinagar what to do and where to go, finds my experience in any way useful, this book will have more than served its purpose.

The photographs, though far from doing justice to the country, may perhaps induce some who think Cashmere too far away—and being inaccessible by rail therefore without modern comforts—to take a trip they will never regret.

A.P.

1 *March*, 1920.

CONTENTS.

LIST OF ILLUSTRATIONS.

LIST OF ILLUSTRATIONS.

MAPS.

Three Weeks in a Houseboat.

CHAPTER I.

IN calling this little book "Three Weeks in a Houseboat" I have made a mis-statement, for it was not a houseboat, properly so-called, but a "dunga" which was my home for three weeks in Cashmere.

There are houseboats in Cashmere which would dare to compare very favourably with the best on the Thames; also very simple houseboats, dunga houseboats and the modest dunga.

A dunga is a very large decked-in punt, about 70 feet long and 6 to 8 feet wide, tapering very considerably at either end; on this there is a structure of a light wooden frame covered, roof and sides, with thick reed matting. I will describe my own in detail and hope thereby to convey an idea of a dunga with its comforts and discomforts, for though dungas vary somewhat in their internal arrangements, they are, on the whole, built on similar lines.

In appearance it looks like a very long hayrick on a punt or an elongated Noah's ark made of reeds. The body is divided up into compartments by partitions of wood and matting, and each opens into the next, curtains taking the place of doors: windows there are none, but the mats which cover the sides roll and tie up if desired, and there are trim white muslin curtains running on cords top and bottom, which when drawn prevent outsiders from looking in ; so that one can open up and air the whole dunga in the morning or close the sun out, as desired, or even, alas ! the rain—for it does rain hard at times.

The matting makes the dunga very cool ; but in windy weather the mats blow about, sometimes very unpleasantly as their lower ends are not attached.

My dunga had seven compartments with a free space of 12 feet in the bows and about 6 feet in the stern : the first compartment was a porch about 7 feet long in which were three or four easy chairs ; the second was 3 feet long and had cupboards on either side for crockery, stores, &c.; then came the living room, 8 feet by 6 feet, on a slightly lower level, the furniture consisting of a small table, four chairs, two bracket shelves and a tiny rush table for books, &c. The fourth room, a bedroom with a charpoy—or wood-framed bed with six legs with straps of cloth laced across it—a small table and a chair ; the fifth like it but a little smaller with a very weak four-legged charpoy ; beyond this was the bathroom and lavatory—the bath a zinc one about 3 feet long—and beyond that a little empty compartment about 4 feet long.

The sitting room and bedrooms had carpets or rugs on the floor, and there were visible attempts at making the rooms look comfortable.

Native dungas, i.e. dungas used by natives, have usually only two or three large compartments, and their occupants, usually very numerous, recline or sleep on mats on the floor.

The simplest houseboat is built somewhat on the same plan as the dunga, except that it is entirely of wood, and that the roof over the porch is flat and has a low rail round it, and on this one can sit, access to it being given by a light stairs.

The dunga has two great advantages over the houseboat: first, it is very much lighter and can be poled or towed with much less labour and can go in shallower water, often a great advantage; also, owing to the mats on its roof and sides, it is very much cooler, for when the sun strikes the sides of the houseboat the temperature inside soon rises: against this in cold, wet, or very windy weather the houseboat is much more comfortable, most being fitted with a stove, some also with glass, and wire fly-proof windows.

It it also not hard for the evil disposed to rob a dunga at night, as they can approach quite noiselessly by land or water, lift up the mats and help themselves. This, however, I believe rarely happens.

A dunga houseboat is built just like a dunga only of wood instead of mats, or rather it is like a houseboat except that it has no second storey or roof platform.

With a dunga or houseboat there is a cook-houseboat: like the dunga but only two-thirds its size, without partitions or with only one partition to shut off the kitchen. In this the cooking is done and the personnel sleep, except such as may sleep at either end of the dunga for its safety.

Also to complete the outfit one has a very small punt built on the same lines, pointed at either end for getting about quickly when the dunga is made fast. This small punt is called a shikara.

When you hire a dunga the usual charge for which is from Rs. 30 per month furnished, you get thrown into the bargain the owner or lessee and his family under the heading of "boatmen." His sons of any age, wife and daughters according to the rules of the game being boatmen. The youngest "boatman" on my dunga was a cheery tot of four to five years.

If you have not a *bearer* you can engage a Cashmiri for Rs. 15 a month, with an extra allowance for food of 2 annas per day when away from Srinagar. It is advisable to come to an understanding about this when engaging the bearer.

From what I have seen of the jealousy of Cashmiri, who are mostly Mohammedan, towards Indian bearers, very often Hindus, I should recommend you to get a Cashmiri, even if you have brought a Hindu bearer with you, for though they may not be such good servants, besides their own language they usually speak English and Hindostani, and knowing the country very well can act as guides.

Then you want a *cook and Khansamah.* You can hire one for Rs. 18 per month; and for a stipulated sum, varying from R. 1 to R. 18 per day, he provides all local produce, as milk, butter, bread, eggs, vegetables, meat, poultry, &c., while you furnish the groceries, i.e. tea, sugar, jams, oatmeal, flour, oil, &c., &c.

If there are several in the party the Khansamah ought to feed you for less than a rupee per day, but that will depend on what you want supplying.

Cook and Khansamah, usually one and the same, are only too pleased to buy your groceries for you, unless your Cashmiri bearer has already shown you he can do so better, for there are considerable pickings to be made from that undertaking.

From my own experience I would advise that the cook or boy be made to initial an account of any money advanced towards pay or purchase of stores, and to make them produce the tradesman's account of their purchases, for some are arrant thieves and most of them liars.

A sweeper at Rs. 8 per month is absolutely necessary, and a bhisti for Rs. 5 per month complete the establishment.

Thus the total expenses for a dunga complete for a month would be :—

Hire of Dunga	say	Rs.	35
,, Cook-boat	,,	,,	15
,, Shikara	,,	,,	5
Staff : Boatmen and Crew ..	,,	,,	0
Bearer	,,	,,	15
Cook	,,	,,	18
Sweeper	,,	,,	8
Bhisti	,,	,,	5
		Rs.	101

The dunga is or should be fitted up ready for occupation, with all necessary furniture, crockery and cooking utensils, not of course with bedding, towels, &c.

Before starting on my trip I will give a short description of my household, which consisted of the boatman, his wife and family of six, the khansamah, or cook and purveyor, the sweeper and bhisti, and my servant or boy.

The boatman was a nice looking, tall man of about 36 to 40; his eldest son, a quiet tall boy of 16, always very obliging; the second son, about 14 years old, a rather surly youth; and the third, a bright cheery boy of 12, who looked upon his work as a great joke and was always eager to take me out in the shikara.

The boatman's wife—his second—and mother only of the girls, was a nice-looking woman, and though brought in under the head of boatman, chiefly confined herself to household duties, but did help to paddle the cookhouse when necessary.

The eldest daughter, a bright hard-working girl of 10, besides helping her mother in her work and tending her two younger sisters, did real hard tracking and paddling for the cook boat.

The next, a little tot of about 4, a very pretty little thing, was the life of the boat, always laughing and smiling, hopping and dancing about and trying to help either when tracking or rice-pounding, or in any other way, even to looking after her baby sister of 8 or 9 months, the last of the family.

It was a very happy family, the boys being devoted to their half-sisters, especially the two smallest. The little girl's usual costume, besides the head-dress cap and large ear-rings, necklace, anklets, &c., was a short gown to the knees, except when we got near fashionable centres when the little mite had to wear bloomers as well.

The cook, a middle-aged, ugly, one-eyed man, confined his energies solely to purveying and cooking for me, which he did very well, making scones when fresh bread ran out which would have delighted a Scot, but he never did any other kind of work that was outside his contract, or what he considered beneath him. His kitchen was at one end of the cook-boat on which were fixed mud ovens, &c., and there he reigned supreme.

The *Bhisti* existed in theory, that is to say, his pay was drawn and his work was done, but he did not materialise: so there was less crowding in the cook-boat.

Next the *Sweeper*, very necessary and rather difficult to obtain, as his work is not everybody's choice. The young man who filled the billet for me, got my hot bath, &c., and was always most willing to lend a hand tracking or paddling, and his pay was certainly not excessive.

Last and least in my estimation, at any rate, was my *Bearer* or Boy ; he had an ugly olive brown face and apparently his sole object in coming was to get as much out of me by barefaced lying and thieving as he possibly could. He succeeded to a certain extent, but not as much as he thought he would. His duties were to act as valet and wait at table, &c.; of the first of these he had not the faintest idea, but had fairly civilised manners, kept clean, outwardly at least, and knew the country well, so served his purpose.

My boatman was the owner of the whole outfit, but my bearer, who owned one houseboat and was building another, said the boatmen were not generally the owners, but men put in by them or men who had rented the boats.

CHAPTER II.

AS a kind and grateful Government had given us mortals, worn out with twelve months in a parched flat plain with little vegetation, a clear month in India in 1917, conveying us to any place we chose to go to free of charge, I decided to pass my leave in Cashmere, and, after spending a couple of days in Bombay to refit, got the 2.25 p.m. train on the 15th May for Rawal Pindi.

Though the weather was hot and the carriages crowded the ride was not unpleasant, and though we lost an hour or two during the second day, we steamed into Rawal Pindi after our 50 hours' run exactly on time at 4.50 p.m.

A motor, for which I had wired from Bombay, was awaiting us, and, after a visit to Danjebhoy's Office (the owner of the car) to settle up, we sped away at 5.30 p.m. for Murree, over 39 miles distant and up some 5,000 feet—Pindi itself being 1,790 feet above sea-level. For the first 16 miles or so the road flat, broad and good and very straight, bordered by shady trees, and we certainly exceeded any speed limit that might exist, for we had a powerful machine and needed it for the long steep climb to come ; then we climbed over the foothills, sank again and then started to rise in earnest, each turn gave us new and beautiful extensive views down and over the cultivated valley ; the vegetation changed as we rose, deciduous trees giving place to deodars and pines and the air was beautifully scent-laden and cool. With the dark at 7.30 we reached our destination, and were pleased to have taken coats with us as it was quite cold on the ride.

We spent the night at Sunnybank Hotel and after two days and two nights in a train appreciated the comforts, including the fire, of the Hotel.

Next morning we were off by 8, for our run of 159 miles to Srinagar :—

Rawal Pindi			
to Murree	37	miles —	37 miles.
to Kohala	27½	,,	
Dulai	12	,,	
Domel	9	,,	
Garhi	13½	,,	— 62 miles.
Chenari	16	,,	
Rampur	31	,,	
Baramula ..	16	,,	— 63 miles.
Srinagar	34	,,	— 34 ,,
Murree to Srinagar ..			159 miles.

After a short rise we topped the ridge and started our long descent to the River Jhelum. The view on this side was very grand, for straight over the valley North and East were the gigantic snow-capped Himalayas with some of its loftiest peaks standing out ; though the country close around and the valley at our feet, through which the Jhelum rushed, were not as pretty as the view West from Murree.

PLATE II.

Domel, from the suspension bridge.

Ox carts waiting for the evening.

We soon left the pine belt behind for shrubs and small trees, passing through several villages where post horses were kept for those going by tonga, also long lines of laden carts, whose large white oxen were lying sleepily chewing their cud or feeding. It struck one as strange that these oxen should always be resting, as also the few herds of camels, till one learned that so as not to impede the fast traffic on the roads, horse-drawn light vehicles and motors, and to avoid accidents the slow traffic was only permitted to move at night.

At Kohala we were down almost at river level and crossed the Jhelum over a fine bridge and were in Cashmere. Here were the Customs, and after making sundry statements as required in several books, as the Medical Officers are very particular, and paying divers fees we were allowed to proceed.

This—the signing in a book—was our first experience of one of the institutions of the country of which we were to see so much during our stay.

From Kohala our road, rising and falling, lay alongside the river, a boiling torrent, a hundred yards or so in width, down which the deodar logs were being hustled and tossed about from miles up above; some having found their way into back-waters were floating lazily, others spinning round in quiet eddies, while many were piled up in heaps in the shallows.

After a run of 21 miles from its boundary, or 51 from Murree, we stopped for a short time at Domel (2,200 feet), a very pretty village, where the Jhelum forms a right angle, coming down now from the East and joined here by the Kishenganga from the North. A fine suspension bridge spans the Jhelum and the view from it over towards the old Sikh fort, which controlled the junction of the two rivers, was very fine.

After more book-signing and further fees we were off again, following up the river, rising and falling and rising again along a fine road, kept continually in repair, often cut out of the rock of the cliff and sometimes tunnelled through it. Vegetation was dense even here ; where streams flowed out of the hill side along the road, or trickled down the rocks on the shady side, maidenhair ferns grew in profusion. The whole ride was a continuous source of pleasure. About noon we stopped at Garhi, 62 miles from Murree, and had lunch at the Dak Bungalow which was stood covered with roses in its pretty garden, where roses, hollyhocks, and other familiar friends flourished. The Bungalow faced the wild bare hills across the torrent, here spanned by a very frail suspension bridge. The river is narrower here, a torrent all the way through the gorge from below Rampur. Near Chenari we passed by a pretty waterfall which came down on our right and, soon after, the picturesque village of Uri with its old fort, high above the road. Nearing Rampur the hills receded and the slopes were covered with deodars as was the level glade beyond, through which we crossed, passing a ruined temple and the large electric power works, whose overhead cables accompanied one a long way on one's journey. The power is obtained from an artificial fall of water brought several miles in a large wooden flume, which followed the road on one's right.

The whole road up to Baramula, 63 miles from Garhi, was very interesting and pretty; we skirted round that town, past some very busy stableyards and Khans, and then entered into a splendid motor-road to Srinagar, bordered nearly the whole length of 35 miles by very tall white barked poplars, rather too closely planted to let one get good views. The land was mostly cultivated with or being prepared for rice, any uncultivated ground being covered with a small iris, while here and there were big clumps of a large white, mauve or purple kind.

Before us, to the South, we got occasional glimpses of snow caps, and as we neared our destination a view through the trunks of the lofty poplars of a small hill rising out of the plain, crowned with a picturesque fort, which commanded Sringar and the flat country at its feet.

About 6 o'clock we ran through a part of the old town, and wandered about through the beautiful and open European quarter to find the Office of the Motamid-Darbar, whose head clerk kindly got us a dunga with its complement of servants complete. We were lucky in securing the dunga as Cashmere, being in favour this year, there were few to be had. As it was now dark we made hurried arrangements for food, &c., and were poled from the river into a canal in the Chenar Bagh. The dunga looked nice and comfortable and as the cook was quite good we felt in luck.

Srinagar is 5,250 feet above the sea, so the nights were cold, as were the few days it rained, and we were very thankful we had brought warm clothing and thick coats.

The Motamid-Darbar, an official of the Maharajah, at whose office in Srinagar all visitors should register their arrival and departure, has a sort of information and advice bureau which I advise the visitor in his own interest to consult fully on any subject for which he requires information or help. Licences for fishing and shooting, and information about the best districts where these can be obtained, and guides and shikaris are all supplied if desired.

The great advantage of getting servants, boatmen, &c., from the Motamid-Darbar is that, in case things turn out unsatisfactorily, a complaint soon brings redress, and also that the servants, &c., obtained from him knowing this and fearing to lose further jobs or recommendation, are more careful and as honest as they must be.

It is best to wire or write in advance to the Motamid-Darbar or to some responsible merchant to secure the dunga or houseboat beforehand, as when one arrives just before dark, the usual time of arrival, there is little time to get things done comfortably, and much confusion, should you even have the luck to get a houseboat at all. There is only one hotel in Srinagar, a very good one I believe, but that is usually full, as are its grounds, with guests under canvas, and the prospects of getting into it without previous notice are extremely small.

If you get a houseboat through a merchant, agent or banker, as he may style himself, he generally hangs on to you and tries to supply you with all you want, and a great deal more you don't and can never have any use for, whereas by going to the Motamid-Darbar you are free to patronise whom you will.

On my arrival I had a little trouble with one merchant, whose reputation was not above suspicion, and on suggesting that the affair be referred to the Motamid-Darbar was troubled no more in the matter.

Once in your boat, though you arrive after dark the attack will be postponed till dawn, you are besieged and all your stay in Srinagar you will be stormed by traders of every kind and description, both from land and water; some are only small pedlars, others touts of the large houses and even the heads of these themselves.

"I don't want anything," "Get out of here," "Go away," and much stronger expressions are met with a humble, "You need not buy only just look," &c., &c. Then you usually fall, and if you do not buy a few small articles from the pedlar's boat, you accept the kindly offer of the tout to row you down to his larger store "just to show you." (It is worth noting on arrival that the merchant's or tout's boatmen expect you to tip them for rowing you: so go in your own shikara and you can then also visit other shops). Then you fall is much more serious, for the heads of the larger houses are the most skilful and persuasive salesmen I have ever met, and the articles they have for sale are very tempting. Often the surrender is unconditional, not even limited by one's bank-balance, for our conquerors are bankers and will negotiate post-dated cheques, &c., &c.

To show their extensive custom the usual ever-present large book is produced where you are shown all the illustrious buyers and others, and after you have made your purchase you write in it your name and order and anything else you can be persuaded to, with the idea of catching any chance acquaintance who may read it.

In ordering things to be made it is advisable to date the order, write the price (that in any case) and also state the time the article has to be delivered : this is very important as you may want civil clothes and also be in a hurry to leave Srinagar for the lakes or shooting and once the order is booked in your writing you are liable for payment and may be kept waiting, often for orders booked after yours, so that you may have to go on without them.

Very good boots and clothes are made here and very cheap, the latter of a good and serviceable homespun ; European flannels and cloths are very expensive as, there being no railway in the country, freight is very costly.

The Maharajah has repeatedly refused to have a line built through this part of his territory, though when at Vernag I saw what looked like a very fine road winding up and over the Mountains to the South by the Bamhal Pass near Vernag, and was told it was for the new railway. Let us hope not. Still the country was so overrun with tourists when I was there that I don't see that the train could bring many more.

I mentioned the " usual and ever-present book," so I must explain. Every trader who comes to you or whom you visit produces a sort of small ledger with names of previous customers and remarks and recommendations by them. So far so good ; but if you go to see any place, the custodian immediately rushes at you with an open book, and asks and presses you to write your name in it, showing you a few famous names of statesmen or generals already there as an inducement, and then suggests in an unmistakeable way that a contribution is expected, and follows you about till he gets one. Or you look at a tank with fish in it in a public place but near a temple ; from apparently nowhere comes a priest with a little grain in his hand or a pie's worth of flat-cake, and throws it to the fish and turns to you with his book, pen and ink.

This habit in its most developed state I found about Islamabad, where in one village I was pursued by three self-styled high priests, each with his book, pen and inkpot, trying to induce me to see his temple or mosque.

Fruit and vegetables are brought to the boat, very good English strawberries in May when I was there, but at English prices ; cherries also are very plentiful and good. Apricots, peaches, plums, apples, &c., all come in their due seasons and are, I believe, excellent.

There are, I believe, good local wines and cider to be obtained here, though my boy bought me one bottle of red and one of white wine which I was quite unable to drink. I think he had bought the cheapest, and charged the highest prices. Hence the quality.

There is a very fine fruit garden a few miles from Srinagar by the pretty village of Thid and just below the Pari Mahal : here fruit—apples and pears and cherries, &c.—are grown on scientific methods and very fine fruit is produced. These orchards belong to the Maharajah.

Srinagar can be divided into two parts : the native town with its narrow crowded streets on either side of the river as it makes a sharp bend and flows north, and the new or European quarter beginning just beyond the first bridge and extending eastwards along the right bank of the river : this has fine broad tree-lined avenues, houses with pretty and shady gardens and broad open stretches of lawn for all kinds of games, shaded by tall poplars and chenars, and a very large polo ground where children and ayahs mostly congregate.

Here also along the river front is a broad promenade, and on it are the Banks, Post Office, European shops and agents, and a few of the more enterprising native shops are opening branches.

PLATE III.

Srinagar, view from lower spur of Takht-i-Suleiman.

Srinagar. Maharajah's Palace on left.

The native houses on the river banks rise sheer from the river, but the first floor is some height above the usual water level, as every year with the melting snows the river rises very considerably, and not infrequently carries away the bridges across it : these bridges having huge square piers of stone and timber. Access to the river is obtained through the narrow streets which at intervals debouch on the river, ending in flights of steps down to the water.

The houses, which are almost entirely made of wood, above flood level, are usually of three stories and very picturesque, the windows often latticed as in Egypt, with the roof of shingles usually covered with grass and flowers growing on it.

The streets, which for an Asiatic town are remarkably clean, are lined with picturesque if not attractive shops on either side. The older mosques have a small pointed sort of steeple, while the newer ones have beautiful domes which glitter in the sun like silver, but which on closer inspection betray their humble origin of flattened-out kerosene oil tins.

Though the official or State religion is Hinduism, the majority of Cashmiris are Mahommedans, the approximate numbers being :—

Mahommedans	2,500,000
Hindus	750,000
Buddhists	40,000
Sikhs	35,000

As a result of the official religion no cattle are killed for food, so no beef, except perhaps tinned, can be obtained in Cashmere.

There was a tale current that fishing in one of the lakes was prohibited, because the soul of some relative of a former Buddhist ruler had migrated to a fish in that lake.

The river in its journey through the town is spanned by seven solid and picturesque wooden bridges on very substantial square piers of stone and logs; from the river, canals run round the Baghs or gardens and to the Dal Lake, the entrance to which is just behind the European quarter.

The great feature of the scene is the endless procession of dungas and shikaras: dungas where native families live and bring their produce and wares to the town, and larger dungas bringing stone, timber, &c., and the busy little shikara moving about everywhere.

In the canals and off the European quarter lie long lines of houseboats and dungas, from the simplest to the most extravagant; and opposite the extraordinary building the Maharajah has for his palace lie several fantastic state-barges.

The great tree in Cashmere on the lower lands is the Chenar or plane tree (*Platanus Orientalis*), which grows to enormous height and girth and great age, and of which the Cashmiris are justly proud.

A "Bagh" generally consists of a flat piece of ground with turf like an old English lawn, shaded by fine chenars. There are, however, a few Baghs which really are gardens of the days of the Moghuls and now properly kept up.

It is in the Baghs along the canals that tents are pitched to pass a few weeks in, and the occupants

PLATE IV.

Takht-i-Suleiman.

Hari Parbat. The Gate.

of houseboats moored to their banks have the tables and chairs from their boat placed under the shade of these giant trees. In the Spring of 1917 these gardens were alive with children of British parents who were unable to return home, as in former years, for the hot season ; but from reports one heard of bygone days, the Baghs did not accommodate British children.

To the East of the European Quarter is a hill some 1,000 feet above the plain, surmounted by a small stone temple and a landmark in the district ; it is called " Takht-i-Suleiman—the Seat of Solomon." The hill is easy to climb and well repays the trouble and the time, an easy hour there and back, for the views as one ascends and from the little temple are superb :

The river Jhelum winding by just below, the whole town laid out before you, the fort of Hari Parbat standing out on its little hill to the North above the outskirts of the town, and the long poplar avenues extending as far as the eye can reach ; at your feet to the South-West, the European Quarter with its large playing-fields, pretty gardens and poplar-lined roads, while to the North-East, from the foot of the hill to the far distance, Lake Dal, reflecting in its still waters the shadow-streaked hills beyond, recalling some of the Scottish lakes ; beyond these again, and framing the view all round, the lofty snow-capped mountains.

On the summit, near the Bhuddist temple, irises and dwarf roses were in flower near a few large cut stones, the probable ruins of a former temple. This little temple is said to be the oldest in the country, dating from 200 B.C. and built by Jalaka, son of Asoka, though the greater part of the temple now standing dates from the Sixth Century A.D., when it was rebuilt by Raja Gopaditya.

There was a celebration of some ceremony in progress when I was there, and the priest told my servant I could enter the building if I took my boots off; being reluctant to do so, I was told I could enter without doing so, so I signed the book, made my present and received a rose, and was shown round the tiny shrine.

Francois Bernier, a Frenchman, who for many years resided at the Court of Aurungzebe as physician, made the journey with that Monarch and his Court to Cashmere and left a diary with his experiences. Of Takht-i-Suleiman he wrote:—
"Opposite to Hari Parbat is seen another hill, on which is also erected a small mosque with a garden, and an extremely ancient building, which bears evident marks of having been a temple for Idols, though named Takt Souliman, the Throne of Soloman. The Mohometans pretend it was raised by that celebrated King when he visited Cashmere."

As we proposed visiting the Fort Hari Parbat, we did as advised, went to the Motamid-Darbar and got permission and an authorised man to come with us on the morrow. So at 9 a.m. the following day we started off in a tonga to see the fort; our way took us through the town where vegetables

PLATE V.

Fort Hari, Parbat.

Hari Parbat. Fort from above.

were cultivated on a very "intensive" system and each garden was irrigated with its own well with pole and bucket. The pole is about 9 feet high with a weight on the end nearer the fulcrum and a bucket on a rope at the other. When not in use the pole is upright, the weight bringing the empty bucket up, and the appearance of scores of these poles is rather like that of the masts of a fishing fleet in harbour. To draw water the bucket is lowered by force down the well and the weight is sufficient to bring the full bucket gently up again.

The Fort on top of its island hill looked very imposing, and, having left our tonga outside the walls, we went on foot through the very fine gate in the walls three miles in length which encircle the hill at its foot. These were built by Akbar. In climbing the four hundred feet to the entrance of the Fort, one is rewarded by the views at each halt in the steep climb, but especially by the panorama over the country, town and lake.

The Fort is much smaller than it looks and has two water-tanks and courtyards, with a small temple and gardens. The walls all round are loop-holed, some parts having balconies for the holes. We walked round the Fort on the ridge of its thatched roof; a walk for which the views richly repay the risk. A few sepoys constituted the guard, and the guns, mostly brass, were relics of the past.

From there we went to see the Jumma Masjid, which must have been, and probably by now is, a very imposing building, but as the whole mosque was being rebuilt there was little to see.

Having the afternoon to spare I was rowed across the Jhelum to the Museum, which contained some very fine shawls and a few guns ; otherwise it was not very interesting.

For those who come to Cashmere for this, there are a Club, tennis-courts and a small golf ground.

I had visited several shops in the hopes of seeing the workers, but presumably as I was not a purchaser I was not shown them.

There is a very fine wood carver, with excellent carving on first-class material, but he charges about one-third more than others as good as he : the papier maché articles in his shop were extremely beautiful and tasteful, some looking like fine china vases ; but it always struck me that papier maché and wood were such inferior and worthless materials to decorate with such beautiful painting.

The shawls, old bronzes, &c., &c., were extremely attractive, and it was only by promising to come again on my return to town that I got away with a whole skin.

I had decided to go up river the next morning, but my boatman said that as there was a great Mohommedan festival in two days' time no trackers could be engaged. It may have been so ; I rather fancy the Boy and the boatman wanted to see the festival.

I had armed myself for up-river with enough silver rupees to weigh down the dunga, as I had been told that paper would not be taken outside Srimagar, but I fortunately found there was very little to spend it on.

PLATE VI.

Lake Dal. On trek.

On Lake Dal. Reflections.

CHAPTER III.

LAKE DAL.

IT was the 22nd May, and the weather as beautiful as one could wish, and to get an early start we decided to get into the entrance of Lake Dal that evening ; so started off for the Gate, as the entrance is called.

Entrance is made up a narrow stream which flows from the lake by the foot of Takht-i-Suleiman into the canal, which receives most of its water from the Jhelum above the city, and the levels of the lake, canal and river vary. After a heavy rain the river rises suddenly and the canals slowly, passage out into the river becomes very difficult and rather risky, the boats having to be towed by extra trackers. In fact, after a rise of the river large crowds are drawn to the canal heads to watch the progress of boats going up stream.

When I approached the Dal Gate the level of the lake was higher than that of the canal, and I had to engage ten trackers, who with much pulling and more shouting got us through about a hundred yards of foaming, rushing water to where the channel widened, when they left us to return to the canal again for fresh patrons. There is always a good supply of trackers at this spot. We then moved on a little into a backwater, and, as it was already dusk, tied up to a bank for the night.

The Dal Gate is a favourite spot for fishermen.

The 23rd opened with a glorious morning, and the snow mountains around were all clear and bright, but by eight they were clouded over for the day. At nine we untied and started for Nasim Bagh at the N.W. end of the Lake.

The Dal Lake is a large sheet of very still water about five miles North by South, and some two miles wide and is for the most part very shallow, reeds, rushes and lilies covering a large portion of its surface : its waters are very dark and extremely clear, and as one passes over it one can see the fish darting about in the green vegetation, at times ten or twelve feet down. The villagers round the West side dig up the water-plants—roots, mud and all—load them on their boats, till there appears to be no reason why they should not sink, convey the material to the edge of the lake, deposit it in shallow water, and make gardens of it : thus gradually reclaiming the lake.

The South-West end has been reclaimed to such an extent that little more than half remains as lake, and this is cut into two parts by a raised road, often over arches, which joins the East side by the Nishat Bagh, at about half the length of the lake : in each half there is a tiny artificial island, with three or four chenar trees.

Our way was along a narrow canal with gardens on either side made of soil from the bottom of the

PLATE VII.

Hasrat Bal. The Ghat.

Hasrat Bal. Ghat during the Fete. Sona Lank in distance.

lake, and bounded by young willows planted on the banks of the reclaimed ground. Horticulture was in full swing, watering being effected in the method already described.

About ten we stopped at the picturesque village of Ranwar, just beyond a very pretty mosque with its two wings and slender spire over the central hall. We halted by the solid bridge and fine landing stairs for my Kansamah to obtain fresh stores. The village was a hive of industry being one of the markets for the produce of the lake.

Passing through the village built on either bank of the canal, we soon reached a good stone bridge and shortly entered the lake by a grand chenar tree at the head of the canal commanding a splendid view across the lake and on either side.

Moving on we reached the very pretty village of Hasrat Bal, with its lofty chenars and long ghat of over 300 yards, teeming with life.

Just beyond the village we ran the bows of the dunga ashore by a large chenar and tied up, the cook-boat coming next, followed soon by the shikara with the cook and his new purchases.

The grass here down to the edge of the lake and right away on to the next little village about a mile off and everywhere under the chenars was like fine lawn-turf.

About 200 yards beyond me was one of the famous Baghs of the lake, Nasim Bagh ("Garden of Bliss") which was built by the great Akhar, but the terraces, except for a few grass-grown ruined walls, have disappeared, and little remains to show its former grandeur, and now it is a grove of some hundreds of very fine chenars planted in long rows, dead ones having been replaced by young trees. A peculiarity of these trees is that their trunks often become quite hollow to a height of 10 or 12 feet from the ground and open several feet, the tree to all appearances being perfectly healthy.

These afford capital shelter in case of a storm; and in case of emergency, if properly cleaned, would afford far from uncomfortable shelter for the night.

In this Bagh this peculiarity was particularly conspicuous as by far the greater part of the old trees were hollow.

Just behind my "pitch" was a large modern fruit garden, well irrigated and with rows of banksia roses and flowering shrubs on the end towards the lake, and two hundred yards further off was an isolated, desolate little post office in a hollow on the sward halfway between the two villages.

There were several houseboats here already and others gradually arrived for the great fete on Friday, the 25th.

In the afternoon, with the shikara I went for a trip up the Telbal river at the North end of the lake for about 2 miles. The ground here was thickly planted with willows and we passed a few villages of farmers with fine substantial houses. Returning we got a view of Mount Mahadev (13,000 feet) standing out on the East and to the South-West a long snow range.

PLATE VIII.

Ranwar. The Mosque. My boatman in foreground.

Hasrat Bal. Arriving for the Fete.

We called in at the Chenar Island or Sona Lank (Golden Island), a little artificial island about 40 yards square with a tree at each corner and a raised terrace in the centre about 20 yards square. One of the chenars was hollow and the cavity fitted with a door and lock. We returned to the dunga and in the dusk wandered into the picturesque and very busy village with a fine mosque, and bought a very substantial easy wicker chair for 4½ Rs., and learned later that my " honest " Boy had retained a considerable part even of that.

24th. Up at 6.30 to find an overcast sky and light rain which kept on till nine, when I went to further explore the village. The picturesque mosque with its painted facade and grass-grown roof has a large open space before it up to the edge of the lake, where is a large flat stone for preachers ; behind the mosque was a large open grass space wider than the mosque and for a short distance bounded on either side by houses, but beyond extending far into the open country.

I was welcomed by a number of priests and shown over this interesting mosque. The main room was rather small and its roof was supported by four tall carved walnut columns, while the walls of the main and small rooms adjoining were covered with votive pieces of valuable tapestry or shawls about 3 to 4 feet by 6 to 8 feet in size. In one room was a closed recess wherein the relics were kept; one, I believe, claims to be a hair of the Prophet.

Of the wings on either side of the mosque proper,

that on the South was for the housing of pilgrims, while the other was a bathing place and sudatorium; the room had a very low ceiling supported by nine columns and part of its floor was heated from below, while there were water baths attached.

The priests refused a contribution to their funds that day as they preferred me to give it the next to swell the receipts of the big festival; but, alas for the plans of mice and men! in the enormous crowd about the mosque next day I never got near the priests.

In spite of the light rain I decided to paddle over to Nishat Bagh, so with the boys and the sweeper started off in the shikara; the boys were always full of fun and spirits and treated the whole trip as a sort of holiday and paddled hard and spurted out of pure animal spirits. Crossing the lake we passed boats busy gathering weeds and mud for gardens, others in groups of sixes or eights fishing together with nets, but the most picturesque was the solitary spear fisherman, who, standing in his small boat, his sunburnt body clad only in a loin cloth, motionless with arm and spear upraised, looked like a bronze statue, and on this dark smooth water the reflection was as clear as the object.

The green weeds below teemed with life and these fishermen make a fair living by their take though they sell the fish for very little, for we bought two weighing about half-a-pound for half-an-anna (½d.).

To reach Nishat Bagh one passes from the North part of the lake through an arch carrying the raised

PLATE IX.

Nishat Bagh from the Bridge.

PLATE X

Nishat Bagh. From Garden House looking up.

Nishat Bagh. From top terrace looking down towards the Lake.

road, already alluded to, which cuts the lake in two and strikes the East side half-a-mile North of the Bagh, while another spur of the same road leads to a village just South of it, thus enclosing a small lake. Exactly facing the arch is the garden whose lower wall with its garden houses lie along the road close to and parallel with the shore and are usually reflected in its quiet waters.

The garden was really beautiful: beautiful roses in large bushes grew profusely and flowering shrubs of great variety abounded. It rose in a number of long and broad terraces, some 10 to 12 feet above each other, and from a fine building on the highest a cascade started, falling from terrace to terrace down steep iron gratings, which gave each cascade a design, and flowing through the middle of each terrace in a channel with rows of small fountains. There were paths at either side of the garden bordered by bright-coloured flowers, as phloxes, carnations, geraniums, stocks, &c., and the whole garden was beautifully shaded by giant chenars.

On the lowest terrace there was a charming two-storied garden house, prettily painted inside, but sadly neglected, from which an exceedingly fine view was obtained. Just below was the small lake with a shikara gliding along it, then the raised road and arch, the main lake beyond with the fortress-crowned Hari-Parbat rising above the willows and trees on its West shore, and far away beyond, the lofty Himalayas with their snow-caps.

The garden was built by Jehangir about 1620 A.D. Here, as everywhere in this country or at least in the lowlands, large starlings, Myna birds and hoopoes abounded and were extremely tame and brightened the country by their presence.

Photographs can give but a poor idea of the beauty of these gardens as they are too large and too flat for a really representative picture to be obtained.

Rain began to fall so we hastened across the lake, reaching our floating home just before the storm burst.

I was much struck by some waterbirds which were not uncommon on these lakes, and which, when standing on the lily-leaves, very strongly resembled silver pheasants in colour and build; they had a long curved white tail which, when swimming, formed an arch on the water, and they had a peculiar cry like a cat, viz., mi-aow-ow.

After a stroll at sunset on the velvet turf under the chenars of Nasim Bagh, with a view through their arches of the now rose-coloured snow-caps, I returned to my dunga for the night, having given order to move off before dawn to the little Sona Lank, where I hoped to find a little peace, as with the fast assembling dungas and houseboats I saw that the shore by Nasim Bagh would be no place for a peaceful man. As quiet gradually reigned one heard prayers rising from the dungas around, till one by one these too ended in the silence of sleep.

PLATE XI.

Nishat Bagh. View from garden. Hari Parbat in distance.

Nishat Bagh. View through Garden House.

Friday, May 25th, broke a glorious day with the usual clear view of nearer and distant mountains, only too soon to be clouded over again. By 5 a.m. we were off to the little Chenar Isle where we tied up facing Hasrat Bal, and at 9.30 a.m. moved off in the shikara to see Shalimar-Bagh (Royal Gardens), and by this time the lake was alive with dungas and punts peopled by Cashmiris going to visit the various Baghs before the fete or going direct to Hasrat Bal. .We paddled up a narrow creek at the North-East end of the lake, already crowded with light-hearted holiday-makers. In some of their boats there were from 50 to 60 people, all in the best of humours.

A pretty walk of about a mile along this channel bordered by willows and other trees and thronged on both banks by men, women and children in their best and brightest garments—some parties having with them dancing girls beautifully dressed—led to the village of Shalimar through which one went to the beautiful garden of that name.

The garden was entirely walled-in and was built by the Emperor Jehangir for his queen Nur Mahal, in the early years of the Seventeenth Century. Like the Nishat Bagh it had a fine background of a lofty mountain range. There were four very large and gently rising terraces with a cascade issuing from under a pretty summer-house just above the highest terrace and flowing down through the middle of the terraces, some of which had sunk gardens, and the borders of all the paths were well laid out with flowers, geraniums, verbenas, phloxes, &c. In the middle of the third terrace, standing in a square basin with fountain jets and with water flowing round it, was a fine temple-like building with open sides, the roof supported by fine black marble pillars. The whole garden was beautifully wooded and shaded by large trees.

Bernier, who had visited all the Baghs, wrote :—
" The most beautiful of all these gardens is one belonging to the King, called Chahlimar (Shalamar Shala-house—Mar, the goddess of Love). The entrance from the lake is through a spacious canal, bordered with green turf and running between two rows of poplars. Its length is about 500 paces, and it leads to a large summer-house placed in the middle of the garden. A second canal, still finer than the first, then conducts you to another summer-house at the end of the garden . . . . In the middle is a long row of fountains, fifteen paces asunder, besides which there are here and there large circular basins or reservoirs, out of which arise other fountains . . . . The summer-houses are placed in the midst of the canal consequently surrounded by water . . . . They are built in the form of a dome and encircled by a gallery, into which four doors open, two looking up or down the canal, and two leading to bridges that connect the buildings with both banks. The houses consist of a large room in the centre, and of four smaller compartments, one at each corner. The whole of the interior is painted and gilt, and on the walls of all the chambers are inscribed certain

PLATE XII.

Shalimar Bagh. Upper Pavilion.

Shalimar Bagh. Lower Pavilion.

sentences written in large and beautiful Persian characters. The four doors are extremely valuable, being composed of large stones and supported by two beautiful pillars. These were found in some of the idol temples demolished by Shah Jehan, and it is impossible to estimate their value. I cannot describe the nature of the stone, but it is far superior to porphery, or any species of marble."

(The doors no longer exist : the material of the pillars is believed to be a black and grey fossiliferous marble).

Moore in his Oriental romance, "Lalla Rookh," used this garden as his principal scene.

We made our way out of the garden by a small gate at the top and for two miles followed the torrent up its well-wooded and iris-studded course through a few tiny villages and past some nicely built houses to Harwan, behind which we looked over large and well cultivated paddy fields, which the River Telbal watered, to Mount Harawar (11,300 feet) in the North. The property round Harwan belongs to the Maharajah and is managed by the officials of his Work and Forests Department.

Just above is the reservoir lake for Srinagar, formed by the building of a dam across the valley : a covered channel takes the water round the mountain slopes behind Nishat Bagh to the City. To ensure the purity of the water huts were removed from and no cultivation is allowed in the catchment area and sheep are not even permitted to graze there.

There is very fine fishing to be had in the lake, but a special licence is required.

Just below the dam we were shown the trout hatcheries, which were extremely interesting and well worth a visit : fish from an inch or so to mighty twelve pounders were separated according to size and requirement into small tanks fed from the lake by one of its overflow streams in its course downhill. My guide informed me that the very large trout were kept for seed !

Back once more to this glorious garden, which with the groups of dignified men in long robes and white turbans strolling along the paths and their families sitting in the shade of the trees looked what it might well have been like some centuries ago.

Though hundreds of people had visited the gardens there were no papers or other debris lying about nor any unseemly noises.

Rejoined my boat and across the lake to my little island, now alive with people and surrounded by boats, which luckily soon left to join the Festival.

I had ordered my Boy to secure me a room overlooking the field where the majority of worshippers assembled, and as the service was to begin at 2 p.m. and the crowd was already great I did not want to land too long before the time, so paddled along the front in my shikara ; but the crowd of dungas was so great that when I wanted to land I had to go nearly a mile beyond the village before we could squeeze our boat's nose in between others and so get to the shore ; and none of them were side on to the shore and in many places were two and three deep.

I then made my way by a quiet back street to what had yesterday been open fields behind the mosque, but was now a densely packed mass of some 50,000 to 60,000 men squatting in long rows facing West, their backs to the mosque, for quite five hundred yards. Round these were women and children sitting in groups and behind them hawkers of all kinds, empty tongas and vehicles of those who had come by land.

The whole crowd with women and children could have been little short of a hundred thousand.

My lying Boy had got no room, but had trusted to chance to find one at the last moment, whereas every house within view was packed on every floor. My tailor from Srinagar tried to help me and took me right round and through the fringe of the crowd finishing up without success near the mosque in a dense crowd. Prayers now began, so I perforce remained where I was ; the enormous crowd of men went through the three outward forms of prayer almost as a man, and the long rows of white turbanned figures standing, kneeling and prostrating themselves, and praying in unison, though very piano, were very impressive, but the effect was a little spoilt by the noise of the hawkers and children.

After the prayers sermons began from different preachers and I passed down to the front of the temple, more densely packed if possible than the fields behind ; here luckily I met a Srinagar merchant who got me a window in a house overlooking the square before the mosque and near the river. It was on the second floor and I had to pass through rooms full of people, who were very deferential, and a window in a fairly crowded room was left entirely to me, and neither here where I took photographs nor at any place or time in the crowd did I receive any but considerate treatment, though on an occasion such as this one could expect the crowd to be fanatical.

From my window I had a grand view: to the left across the square through an opening in the branches of the lofty chenars lay the mosque packed with people and priests, in front of them a sea of white turbans, being addressed by preachers, nearer to me were the booths of pedlars and cooking stalls where cakes of all kinds were made as ordered—(the misty patches in the foreground of the picture were caused by the smoke from the cooking stalls), just below the window a passage up to the field behind the mosque now blocked with women and children, a little to my right the water front with its ghat densely packed, mostly with people bringing up produce for sale, and in the water dungas crowded together extending nine or ten deep into the lake; among these was the usual bathing place, but on this day the pilgrims washed their hands and feet before and after the service.

Soon after the service had ended the crowd began to break up and to flow down the passage below my window and from the square to the river front along which was a crowd going in either direction. In a very few moments there was a dense crowd of pushing humanity, and though some of the younger men were a little rough and attempts were

PLATE XIII.

Hasrat Bal. The Mosque.

Hasrat Bal. The Fete.

made to direct the traffic, not a single person lost his or her good humour, nor was there any rowdyness or unpleasantness of any kind. I don't think I ever saw so orderly or so good-natured a crowd.

About 4 p.m. the dungas and houseboats were well on the move and the lake seen from this village was a dense mass of boats, many of whose occupants were singing or playing musical instruments, recalling memories of Henley Regatta between the races.

Soon after 5 o'clock I got back to my peaceful and now deserted island, after a most enjoyable day. The snow mountains again showed clear in the sunset behind the still busy village, which later, after dark, looked very gay with its many lights and those of the boats, moored there or afloat, reflected in the mirror-like surface of the lake.

26th. At 5 o'clock next morning we bade farewell to the little isle and laid up for breakfast by the archway near Nishat Bagh. The little lake was fairly full of boats from the festival and in one boat moored on the other side of the arch a dancing girl was performing. Moving on again we were soon in the Lokut Dal or southern half and passed the little island there, Rupa Lank (Silver Island), shortly after which, directing the dunga and cook-boat to await me near the Dal Gate, I got into the shikara with my Boy as guide and two of the boys and making our way through the rushes reached the shore near the village of Thid, where I left a boy in charge of the boat and started inland on a road which joined the main lake-shore road at Thid.

We passed by some very prosperous looking farm-houses, with large cherry gardens, and very fine walnut trees and well laid-out apple orchards. My objective was the Pari Mahal, a massive and very imposing ruin on the side of a hill ; my Boy could tell me nothing about it and my guide book little more, except that it was about 800 years old. As no road or path apparently led to it we made a line across country through various farmhouses and orchards, where for the first time I saw the villagers using fire baskets—little baskets lined with burnt clay in which they carried live embers—then along some 500 yards of covered wooden channel which was bringing the Harwan water to Srinagar, and then up a very steep hillside.

The building must have been very fine, having been substantially constructed in five or six large terraces. There were remains of what looked like cloisters and cells, and there were passages from each terrace to the one above. Two small rooms had remains of frescoes on their walls.

Owing to the slope of the ground it was impossible to take a photograph to give any idea of the grandeur of these ruins. The two here produced give (No. 2) the two lower terraces from below the North-East corner, and (No. 1) the domed part of the highest terrace taken from the South or behind, with Lake Dal spread out below. The ground here was a tangle of wild roses, honeysuckle, irises and shrubs.

I rejoined my dunga by Gagirbal, and returning to Srinagar made arrangements to start on the morrow up-stream.

PLATE XIV.

Pari Mahal. 1. Dome on highest terrace. Lake Dal beyond.

Pari Mahal. 2. The two lowest terraces.

CHAPTER IV.

WE were off by 6 a.m. in almost cloudless weather, out of the canal and soon in the river, which being swollen by recent rains had made the passage through the canal gate rather exciting, the canal being lower than the river, and progress up stream rather slower and harder work.

Two strong trackers had been hired for the purpose at about Rs. 8 each for the journey, as I objected to arrangements of so much per day, time being of great importance with me.

We proceeded " piecemeal " so to speak, that is to say, the dunga was towed by the trackers and steered by the boatman with the help of the elder boy, and these two occasionally relieved the two trackers or would lend them a hand. The cook-boat was in charge of the sweeper, younger son and elder girl and sometimes the tiny mite of a little girl would help with a rope; the shikara was left in charge of the youngest son who usually paddled it.

The distance to Islamabad is about 47 miles by river, but rate of progress depends on the wind and strength of the current, houseboats often taking four days to reach it. Our light dunga scored and in spite of the strong current against us made quite rapid progress and passed many boats en route.

After passing a long line of sumptuous houseboats, moored to the bank, one of which had a third storey or rather two rooms over the second, we cleared the town and had a splendid view up the first reach to the Spill Channel, now nearly dry, but which takes off the flood water from the Jhelum into swampy lakes to the West of Srinagar, from which it flows North-West till it reaches the Haigam Jhil and the South end of the Wular Lake and so back again to the Jhelum. In crossing waterways like the Spill Canal the shikara sometimes took the trackers across and sometimes we took them on the dunga and poled over to the other side, as we used to do when the towing path changed from one bank of the river to the other.

From the Spill Channel the river wound very considerably and the little temple on Takht-i-Suleiman was visible for many hours, first behind, then in front, or at either side of us.

Our first halt was made to visit the tiny Buddhist temple of PANDRATHAN : which is only 1½ miles by road from the canal entrance but over 4½ by river. It lies a little way back from the river and the main road in a depression full of water which will soon hasten its complete ruin by undermining the foundations. It is a small gothic-looking building of stone, about 18 feet square and 24 high, though the apex of the temple is missing ; there are four porches, one at each side, with columns, the whole highly decorated with carving. It is said to have been built about 915 A.D. and to be the only building left of the old town of Srinagar, which then covered the ground around it and which was destroyed by fire some fifty years later.

PLATE XV.

Pandrathan.

Avantipur. Carved Capital.

When on the bank I saw some strolling players in very fantastic costumes waiting under the willows by the river ; the place seemed a favourite picnic place for Srinagar.

Just beyond I noticed that willows were being cut down and also large piles of short willow logs, or rather planks, about 4 feet long and 4 to 5 inches thick and was informed these were going to India to be made into cricket bats.

On the flat country to the South, saffron is extensively cultivated and is a very paying crop.

This way of travelling is most luxurious ; one sits in an easy chair in the porch of the dunga gliding through the water with one's house, dependants and all one's belongings about one, and here the advantage of a houseboat comes in for one could sit on the top and so get a better view over the country, but against that is the disadvantage of slower progress and more trackers.

Early in the afternoon we passed the town of Pampur, and soon after under the picturesque bridge by Kadabal, where was one of the Maharajah's houses and a grove of fine chenars, and at 6 p.m. we stopped for the night under a high bank on the left just beyond a village where a wide canal full of large country boats entered the river, and just below a tiny mosque in a little garden. On landing the priest or custodian of the mosque came out to see we did no harm and to learn our business, but raised no objection to our tour of inspection.

After sunset, with the boys I went fishing down the canal which has the reputation of a good fishing ground.

During the day I noticed numbers of a tiny mauve-lined iris, rather larger than the Spanish, and also a large pale blue bird with grey wings and tail, a Roller, about the size of a large pigeon, emerge from a hole in the sand cliff over the river.

This place has an evil reputation for thieving and though the boys slept at each end of my dunga for safety I did not feel quite safe as anyone from the water or river bank could lift up the matting and help themselves to anything inside. Luckily nothing did happen and early next morning we continued up stream.

I soon landed, with my Boy, on the right bank and walked across country to see the ruins of two Buddhist temples by Avantipur, about half-a-mile apart and apparently both built on the same plan. The larger one to the North has a gateway standing and must have occupied a very large area as shown by the extensive ruins which were mostly overgrown with grass : the smaller one nearer the river has been thoroughly excavated and shows the interesting ruins of what was once a very fine temple with beautiful carvings. There is a shed hard by used as a museum in which among other finds are some small earthenware lamps very like the old Greek and Roman, and just outside the shed is a collection of amphoræ, many of them over 5 feet high and large enough to have hidden Ali Baba and his gay companions. These ruins reminded me very much of the ancient ruined temples of Greece.

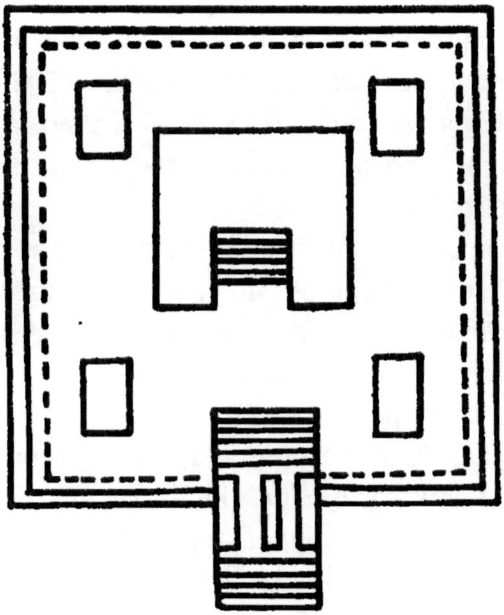

Plan of Temple of Avantipur.

The smaller and excavated temple consisted of a large court about 40 yards square with colonades round its sides, which may have contained cells, supported by trefoil arches; a large central shrine on a stone plinth with a flight of steps up it facing the entrance and a large entrance arch also on a plinth with a large flight of steps on either side;

there were also four smaller plinths which may have been pedestals for images or bases for smaller shrines.

Numerous fragments of beautifully carved stone and fine fluted columns lay about. The soil had luckily preserved the carving for all that had stood above ground was very much weather-worn.

These temples are all that remain of the capital of the King Avantivarma (and called after him Avantipur), who flourished in the latter half of the Ninth Century.

The rest of the day was uninteresting and the sky dull and our progress slow. The houses in this district had a prosperous look, but the large mulberry trees which grew in great quantities along the banks had a very henpecked appearance.

The Rajah's government largely encourage the rearing of silkworms for the large silk factory at Srinagar, and such villagers as are willing to rear the "worms" are supplied with the "seed" as my Boy explained to me and got a fixed price per maund (80 lbs.) for the cocoons.

These cultivators then buy the leaves of sundry standing trees in their neighbourhood from the owners and cull them and the small branches as required. A few days later I saw a very serious fight over the ownership of such branches which drew in the partisans of both parties and was finally settled by all the village joining in.

I notice also all along the bank of the river large herds of cattle—rather small, like Kerry—with very

PLATE XVI.

Avantipur. Ruined temple.

Ruins of Martand.

short horns, also herds of thin small sheep whose lambs ran like greyhounds. At one point on the bank we passed a long thin snake which I concluded to be poisonous from the row the boatman made and the care he took to warn his children; this was the first snake I had seen in Cashmere.

Of butterflies I saw so few that, though a keen collcctor, they left no impression on my memory, probably it was too early for them and the few I saw must have been " hibernators "; some time later near Domel I saw some large blue and black (*P. Ulysses*).

About dusk we tied up by a little village near which were large stacks of mustard in seed, stacks of 4 or 5 tons, and I was told that an oil was obtained from the seed.

This evening, as on most others, I tried my hand at fishing, helped by my Boy and the boys, and with the same unsatisfactory result; still it amused the boys and helped pass the half-hour of twilight.

We were off at dawn next day and about 8 a.m. neared the very pretty town of Bejbehara, a striking feature of which was the log houses on stone foundations. Thc town is well above the river and looks very fine; there is the usual type of heavy wooden bridge across the river and two large chenar Baghs, one on either side just beyond it with magnificent trees. Here we tied up for breakfast and went out to explore. In this Bagh, on the left bank, was one especially fine chenar, 53 feet round the trunk at 3 feet from the ground and the trunk was solid.

Later I took a walk through the town to see a very pretty mosque which contained some very fine carved wood tombs of considerable age, its pillars and ceilings were also carved, and it well repaid the visit ; returning through the town I stopped to buy some silver ornaments at a small silversmith's where they were making and mending bracelets, &c., and soon the shop entrance was blocked by crowds of curious spectators.

Arriving back at the Bagh I was greatly annoyed to find my fleet had already sailed and was out of sight, so we took a short cut across the fields which were well cultivated: fields of blue flax, others of maize and other cereals and lots of small red poppies. Having re-embarked we reached, about 1 p.m., our destination, Khanabal, the furthest navigable point on the Jhelum which here splits into, or, more properly speaking, is made up here from numerous streams. Passing under the bridge, as the best sites were already occupied, we tied up just beyond and under a bank some 20 feet high, on which stood the Dak Bungalow, and about one mile from the the outskirts of Islamabad or Anantnag.

Khanabal is joined to Islamabad by a raised and almost straight good road, bordered by fine poplars with paddy fields behind extending to the foot of the distant hills and now in the early stages of preparation and sowing in full swing : this last word very accurately describes the graceful, if elementary and rather dirty, method of stirring the mud with their feet preparatory to planting the rice shoots.

PLATE XVII.

Bejbehara. The Bagh, my dunga and cook boat by bank and shikara in mid-stream.

Bejbehara. Rice Milling.

A man with a strong stick in each hand and well planted in the ground at arm's length, swings his left foot across through the mud in front of the right one and swings it back and forward advancing a pace, then does the same with the right foot and so on, his body turning gracefully with each movement, the sticks supporting him. When, as often happens, three men are working together in line and in step the effect is quite pretty.

Islamabad is a long straggling town at the foot of a hill, about 500 feet above the plain but nearly 6,000 above the sea, which rises precipitately from behind the mosque at the far end of the square and is a very busy place, though it has no local industry ; its prosperity it owes to its situation on the main road from the Punjab to Kashmir, Ladakh and the districts to the North. There is a good school here as in most large villages and towns, and English is taught, and when I first passed by the teachers and Post Office officials, all natives or Indians, were playing lawn tennis.

A tributary of the Jhelum, the Lidar, with very tortuous winding and many smaller sub-tributaries, flows along the southern side of the town and joins the river by Khanabal.

Soon after arrival I walked over to and through the town to the temple and caravanserai with its large fishponds under the stately chenars at the foot of the hill : from these ponds the water flows with a slight fall into a basin and thence to a pretty stream ; the basin and stream being very largely used for laundry purposes.

Seeing me interested in the fish the chief priest, evidently on the look out for prey, came out of the temple, bought an anna's worth of cakes, ready on sale for the purpose, and threw fragments into the pond where there were trout in thousands, some being very large, over 2 feet long. I was then taken to see the temple with a hot sulphur spring and bath in its grounds ; the inevitable book was then produced and a few distinguished names shown as a bait.

Returning to my boat I found another dunga with friends alongside mine and later we returned to the town and climbed the steep hill behind it, and were well rewarded for our pains by the magnificent view. Just below, the town, nestling in its orchards with green fields beyond them, looked not unlike a little English country town, but beyond were paddy fields extending right up to the foothills, with here and there shaded roads running across the country, and the giant peaks of Kolahoi (17,900 feet) which showed up very clearly to the North seemed very much closer.

Having arranged for a tonga for the morning we returned home, but, owing to the high banks and sharp turns of the here narrow river, there was little air, so we shifted further up and to the other bank, but with little success : there are no good stations for boats here.

The 30th. Off with the tonga soon after 6 o'clock, with my Boy as guide an interpreter ; back to and through Islamabad and on some five miles along a

PLATE XVIII.

Vernag. The approach.

Archibal.

shaded road and through several small hamlets to the pretty village of Archibal, shaded by giant trees with a stream meandering through its length alongside the road, then to a park shaded by fine chenars where a party was camping in the luxurious style of India. Here we left our carriage and entered the extremely pretty small walled-in garden, which had a stream flowing through the grounds and several pretty summerhouses ; close against the further garden wall rose a steep hill clad with deodars and passages from the garden led on to the hill itself from which the usual fine panorama is obtained.

Close by was another trout-hatchery and the district was under State management.

Francois Bernier, who visited these gardens about 1670, wrote the following of them : " I turned a little from the high road for the sake of visiting Archival, a country house formerly of the Kings of Kashmir."

" What principally constitutes the beauty of this place is a fountain whose waters disperse themselves into a hundred channels round the house which is by no means unseemly, and throughout the gardens. The spring gushes out of the earth with some violence, and the water is so abundant that it ought rather to be called a river than a fountain.

" The garden is very handsome, laid out in regular walks and full of fruit trees—apple, pear, plum, apricot and cherry. Jets d'eau in various forms and fishponds are in great number and there is a lofty cascade which in its fall takes the form and colour of a large sheet 30 or 40 paces in length, producing the finest effect imaginable, especially at night when innumerable lamps are lighted under it.

"From Archival I proceeded to another royal garden (Vernag) embellished much in the same manner. One of its ponds contain fish so tame that they approach on being called, or when pieces of bread are thrown into the water. The largest have gold rings, with inscriptions, through their gills placed there by the celebrated Nur Mahal, wife of Jehungir, grandfather of Aurungzebe."

In this district tobacco was largely cultivated and vegetables of many kinds; mustard and of course rice very extensively.

On my return I found my friends starting for a week's tramp in the hills North of Islamabad, picking up their boat again at Bejbehara, and I greatly regretted my arrangements did not permit me to go with them as the country is extremely fine.

A very nice short trip of three or four days from Islamabad via Bawan, the Lidar Valley to Pailgam and back to the river at Bejbehara. Bearers, ponies and equipment can be obtained at Islamabad and one can ride or walk.

About 1.15 p.m. I drove through the North branch of the town, for the hill runs into it like a wedge, past the well-kept Zenana Mission Hospital, and over 3 miles of the worst roads in the country, past a fine modern school standing alone on the

PLATE XIX.

Vernag. Ruined Palace.

On the road to Harivan.

green slopes of a hill, where I was attacked by the first high priest with his book, who had been lying in ambush for visitors going to the lovely village of Bawan, a little further on, nestling under a group of enormous chenars and so shaded as to preclude any attempt of photography. To the right of the road as one enters the village are two mosques, pilgrim houses and two large tanks into which springs flow and then, overflowing through stone-lined channels, pass round and over a lovely greensward to the left under the trees on a terrace, of which the supporting masonry was mostly in ruins, and below this flowed a stream from the Lidar into which these springs fell.

Here two more high priests, so at least they styled themselves, made for me with their books, while a fourth soon joined as I started on foot along the road to see the caves of BAUMAJO, about 2 to 3 miles further on. As the last was the priest of one of the rock hewn temples, I took him as guide to be rid of the rest. One cave into which I went with torches some 50 or 60 yards, though the cave extended a considerable distance further, had a sort of chamber on one side, where a hermit resided some centuries ago; its entrance was 20 feet above the road. The next was some way further on and about 60 feet up the side of the montain and had a doorway carved out of the rock and a carved shrine a little distance inside.

From the doorway one got a splendid view across the Lidar Valley to Mount Kolahoi with its double peak, some 40 miles away.

I here gave my priestly guide a small gratuity, which so pleased him that he remained my guide for the rest of the day to the exclusion of all others.

These Buddhist priests are educated and refined-looking men and it seemed a pity and a shame that they should be reduced to touting for tips. My Boy being a Moslem scoffed at them.

After a grateful rest in the deep shade of the trees at Bawan, for the day was very warm, we retraced our steps and passed the school, went up a steep road which crossed the falls of a canal which supplies water to the Islamabad district; the town being visible from this height, about 4 miles away.

Just over this bridge were the imposing ruins of MARTAND in its splendid setting, which reminded me of that of a temple in the Morea, and the ruins themselves had many an old Greek feature. Behind them to the North-East are the foot-hills with the torrent rushing by, all beyond to the East and the South the snow-crested mountains, and in front the bare plateau sloping gradually away to the West, so that the temple stood out alone in its grandeur.

It is much the same design as that of Avantipura only larger and grander and must have been a noble structure, for though the carvings and stone are much weather worn the ruins are still very imposing.

The quadrangle enclosing the temple measured roughly 70 yards by 50, and against its walls are the ruins of some 80 small cells; it has a large entrance porch in the West wall. The temple was 60 feet by 38 and consisted of two apartments: the main body or nave and the sanctuary, the latter was quite plain while the nave was decorated with carving. Entrance was effected by a wide flight of steps through a fine trefoil arch which has a small chapel on either side, and on the other three sides of the temple are arches of the same size and design but built up.

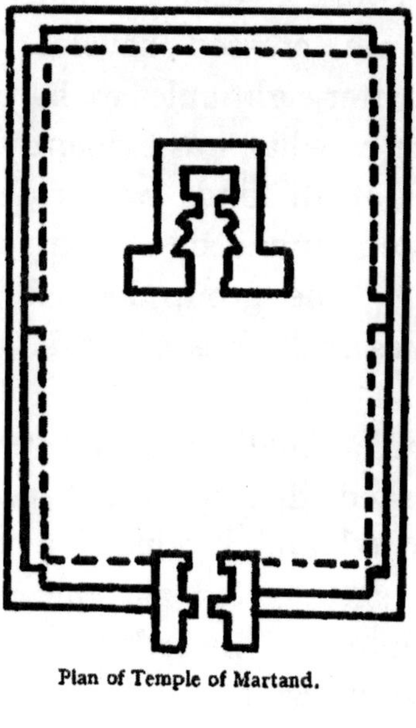

Plan of Temple of Martand.

The temple was probably built in the early half of the Eighth Century by King Lalitaditya and, probably also, erected as a temple of the Sun.

Another way to do this day's excursion would be to ride to Archibal, then direct across to Martand

and Bawan, and return via Islamabad to your boat. The road between Archibal and Martand is only a bridle path.

May 31st. With a clear sky and bright day I was off early in the tonga to visit VERNAG, seventeen miles to the South. A very pretty ride, passing through a few fair-sized villages under shady trees, by fields of maize and of paddy in various stages from emerald green seed beds to fair-sized plants, and groups of women collecting mustard. Rivulets flowed in a network over the country and in the day's journey we crossed several broad, stony torrent beds. After eight miles we halted at a village to rest the horse at what was evidently the half-way house. Groups of all kinds were assembled before it on some shaded ground by a khan, some arriving, some departing; one group looked like a bridal party, the ladies well dressed and veiled, and all mounted.

While waiting, a small group of strolling players arrived and asked if they might perform. Then five men squatted and produced a weird kind of music, while a sixth acted as policeman and kept the boys of the crowd in order with a large split bamboo, waltzing up to them in time with the music. The two dancers, one an ugly little girl of 14 or so, and the other an ugly man with long black hair, dressed in velvet as a woman, and both were quite graceful in their movements though the man's broad waist told against him. Like most Asiatic dancing this consisted of movements of

PLATE XX.

Vernag. The Tank. The Dak-bungalow beyond.

Archibal. View from centre garden house.

arms, hands and feet and occasional gyrations. The singing was not at all bad.

Our road was the main or trunk road from Jummu and the Punjab, and the whole day we passed groups of people wending their way to Islamabad. There were merchants with mules laden with their goods, tramps of all kinds, ragged Ladakis, long-haired rough-looking hill-people, and long trains of freight bulls and ponies, ladies on horseback, smart looking Punjabis under umbrellas, and later in the day very large herds of large goats of all colours from white to black with very long silky coats.

The village of Vernag is one of the prettiest I have seen here; it is situated at the foot of a fir-clad spur of the Pir Panjal Mountain range with large poplars and shady walnut and chenar trees, and the streams of water running through it, full of fish, flow alongside its main road, and a little to one's right on entering is the long ruined arched wall of the old palace in a frame of greenery. In the brilliant morning sun it was a lovely sight. We outspanned by a large trout-stream near the ruins and were mobbed by the inevitable priests, but avoiding them climbed up the ruins and looked down on the large octagonal tank in which the copious spring rose. The tank was paved all round and each side had a colonnade of three arches or alcoves, of which there were twenty-four in all. The tank would be about forty paces across and a few feet deep, and was alive with countless trout of all sizes up to 12 and 14 lbs. The house or palace was badly ruined but the tank was perfect. Facing the ruins across the road was a long garden with fine shady trees and down its centre flowed a stream from the tank in a broad stone channel spanned by three crumbling summer-houses, and which left the garden in a pretty fall of some twenty feet. The tank and house were built by Jehangir and is said to have been his favourite residence.

A hundred yards to the east of the village was a knoll with beautiful turf and shaded by large trees, and the burnt patches of grass testified to its popularity as a camping ground; but there was a Dak-bungalow a little way above the tank.

Returning to my dunga I took my last walk to peaceful and picturesque Islamabad, and made arrangements to leave as the position of the boat was very hot, 85° in the main room, airless and unpleasant, and my Boy informed me I could do sundry other excursions from Bejbehara where camping was ideal.

I had some trouble in getting him away, as a houseboat he owned was lying here. He had acquired means to buy it by robbing confiding tourists, like myself, as I soon discovered. He had also another boat building, which I saw later on, so apparently acting as Boy when conducted with skill is a paying job, and evidently people here put their money in houseboats, as they do in house property at home.

In my walks through Islamabad and in most places in Cashmere, I was struck by the number of sewing machines in use; almost every single native shop had one, and many of the native dungas.

Just before dark we got off and zig-zagging down stream arrived at Bejbehara and tied up.

June 1st was a beautiful day, spoilt for me by finding that my Boy had lied, for I could obtain no vehicles or horses at Bejbehara to go anywhere, as he had asserted I could. Animals and vehicles would have to be brought from Islamabad. So one of my few remaining days was lost, still it was good to be alive and sit under the glorious chenars, where I also took my meals. Later I crossed to the right bank and in that chenar garden were ruins enough to show that it had once been a garden with houses and not merely a park.

My Boy had lied to me on another head as he had told me that on the 1st or 2nd there would take place at Bijbehara a similar fete to that I saw at Hasrat Bal. On enquiry I could find no signs of a fete at any date in the near future.

I was much interested in the fishing carried on in punts where an enormous semi-circular net on a frame was lowered by a simple device into the river and easily raised again, no bait being used, but nevertheless very successfully.

As much silk was produced here I decided to see how the "worms" were raised and went over two small houses entirely given up to them. The same system prevailed in each.

The silkworms were not in captivity, that is they were not in boxes, but might have roamed over the room or house if they had liked, but were kept chained apparently by their appetite: in other words as long as there was plenty to eat they simply sat tight and ate.

On entering a room and these were roughly 6ft. by 9ft., one noticed three "blocks" on the floor with a clear passage about a foot wide between them for the owner to get about, inspect, feed and clean, and each of these blocks was gray with "worms," thousands of them, and at this time nearly full grown, 2½ to 3 inches long, but all nearly motionless on twigs and small branches, eating, eating and eating.

The mulberry twigs and leaves are laid in regular heaps along the blocks and as eaten up fresh twigs and leaves are placed over the old ones, usually criss-crossed, till a height of a foot or so is finally reached. Nothing is taken away, the dirt falling through the twigs to the ground, and the worms always going up to the fresh food on the top. The paths are kept clean and sometimes the whole block raised a little and the dirt partly removed.

When tired of eating they spin their cocoons among the twigs, and when a block is ready, for they are all of an age in a block, the cocoons are collected and, I gathered, put into hot sand to kill the chrysalis and so prevent them from spoiling the silk by eating their way out.

My host told me he collected about a maund (80 lbs.) of cocoons, these he sold to the state factory,

PLATE XXI.

Bejbehara. Log houses and washing house in river.

Pampur. My boatman's "youngest."

which in spring supplied him with "seed," as my Boy called it, for another crop of "worms."

About 3 o'clock I cast off and the three boats went from side to side of the river often almost broadside on and I had reluctantly to learn that though a very nice, willing and honest man, my boatman knew nothing of steering, and I fancy that is the same with all of them: they just let everything drift. About 7 o'clock we halted and a storm burst over us.

The morning opened with beautiful weather so I paid a second visit to the ruins of Avantipur, which were specially interesting after having seen Martand.

Soon after leaving, a very strong wind rose and my boatman was afraid to proceed from fear of being blown over, so we tied up just above Pampur bridge and opposite a ghat near the Maharajah's house already mentioned. All day, but especially towards evening, women and girls of all ages came down there to the river and carried back water, and that on their heads in very large earthenware jars which it seemed hardly possible that they could lift.

All the villages and towns on the river are well supplied with bathing houses in the river and inland villages have small ones over streams; but still every morning and evening I noticed men and women come to the river bank for a superficial and possibly ceremonial wash of definite parts of their bodies.

Wandering across the rather dilapidated and quaint old bridge with its square piers of heavy logs

I went to see the temple a quarter-of-a-mile back from the river near some fine chenars and some scattered ruins.

The wind having fallen we proceeded down stream till dark and tied up for the night, which we spent to the usual accompaniment of dogs barking and donkeys braying.

PLATE XXII.

The Jhelum above Kadabal: evening.

Srinagar. Above the first bridge. Note line of houseboats.

CHAPTER V.

WE were off by dawn and soon at Srinagar, where we tied up just inside the canal entrance to get away as early as possible after I had learnt when my leave was up and had made further arrangements with my banker, but I had not reckoned on the customs of the country. The day being Sunday the Post Office was closed, so I could get no mail or wire, also the next day, June the 4th, it was closed as that was the Maharjah's birthday, a Buddhist festival and a general holiday, and June the 5th was a Mohammedan festival, so the Post Offices and banks were all officially closed till the 6th! That was three days to wait before I could get any orders or money or letters.

Luckily Messrs. Cox & Co. was managed by people with some sense of what was fitting, and calling there I got admission and found that my wire about leave had luckily got sent there instead of being buried in the Post and Telegraph Office; also before I left, though the Bank was officially closed, business was transacted for officers on leave.

Srinagar was very gay, especially the water, as the Maharajah, having recently arrived, his bright coloured barges were lying near the palace ready for use and a continual stream of smartly dressed natives in fine shikaras, the paddlers in uniform, was flowing from the canals and on the river to the palace.

Before noon I drove out to see the Nishad Bagh via the Munshi Bagh, past the land side of Takht-i-Suleiman just beyond which by the village of Tithar were some deer of the Maharajah in stables. The ride would have been very pretty but for the ever-lasting colonnade of tall closely planted white-barked poplars which practically confined one's view to the road ahead and astern.

These poplars, which are like the Lombardy, give very little shade and during the hottest part of the day none at all down the centre of the road, where most wanted.

The gardens were looking very fine, but the fountains which I had come to see made a poor show, many not being in working order.

Returning I avoided part of the poplar-lined road by going along the lake side of Takht-i-Suleiman, past orchards laden with cherries, also pear, apple and other fruit trees.

In the afternoon I went round the larger shops to settle for the little I had bought and was flattering myself how easily I had got off. But he laughs best, &c., and I returned home with my self-respect greatly diminished and a much lighter purse, and there was worse to follow. Still, what one bought was well worth buying and would not be regretted, but the nasty fact remained that you did not intend to let yourself be persuaded and you had been badly beaten.

For shawls I think Bahar Kkan's is a very good shop and old Bahar Khan père is a delightful old man, as is also Samad Shah, or one of the elder members of that firm, who is the most persuasive salesman I ever met ; you feel as if you both were buying, though unfortunately only one had to pay.

Samad Shah's is a most reliable firm, they, like Bahar Khan, will provide you with houseboats, dungas and servants or anything else you may want, and also act as bankers, and Samad Shah will also get you a good tailor, or bootmaker and his profit comes out of them and you know the people can be depended on. The big wood carvers are young men immaculately dressed, as their profits easily permit, but they have not the courtesy of the elder generation.

Another excellent firm is Abdul Aziz, where both father and son are most courteous, though the older generation here too has the advantage. Here I found first-class wood carving on good seasoned wood—for a great deal of good carving is done on poor wood which soon warps and breaks—and at very reasonable prices. I purchased a very fine desk which arrived home two years later because of the war, but in perfect condition, as it was so well packed. Abdul Aziz has also a wonderful collection of bronze and copper articles, ancient and modern, from all round this region : old coins, arms and ornaments and the useless papier maché. The prices they give they say are their cost to which they add a 10 per cent. commission and these are much below the usual charges elsewhere. It was here I had my greatest fall and my only regret was that it did not come earlier, before I fell elsewhere. I can honestly and heartily recommend this firm.

The craze for papier maché I cannot understand; true the designs and patterns on bowls and vases are very good, and the blotting books and writing cases and other fancy articles are very showy, while the painting and decoration are exquisitely done with the best taste in shading and decoration of keramic art of any period, but all this to my mind is a fearful waste of art and skill on a very base material, often not even papier maché but wood, which is very short lived. Clays for porcelain may possibly not be available, but would I feel surely repay being introduced.

There is a photographer at Srinagar named Vishinati, who develops very well, though his prints might be improved on. Films, &c., can be obtained from him, or from the English chemist near the Club, but I would advise a keen photographer to bring with him as many films or plates as he thinks he may want, as there is a great run on photo-material and he may have to go short.

On the afternoon of my last day at Srinagar I was surprised to find that the chief clerk of the Motamid-Darbar had come to see me, for I had been round to the office to apprise them of my departure and to arrange about payments for the boat, &c. We had a short chat, when he wished me "bon voyage" and left. My Boy asked me why

PLATE XXIII.

Srinagar. In the Chenar Bagh. Note the Deodar logs.

Srinagar, from the seventh bridge.

I had not tipped him: I replied that I had not wished to insult him, and was told it was nevertheless the custom to do so!

Having decided to return from Baramula to Pindi by tonga, as being thus better able to enjoy the scenery, we fixed up with a tonga contractor to have two ready for us, myself and a friend, who was returning with me, at Baramula on a specified day.

One the 5th June I sent the dunga on ahead to await me below the last bridge and completed my arrangements and paddled down a very pretty reach to the seventh bridge, from which looking back a very fine view of the town was obtained in its setting of mountains.

I found my boat by the weir and lock which control the level of the river through the town. The rest of the day we drifted slowly and peacefully, a pleasant change after Srinagar.

In this district I noticed a number of white-headed fish eagles; and at one village saw women grinding corn between two large round flat stones; the upper and smaller one revolving on its centre and grain poured in through a hole in the upper grindstone.

We came across a funeral party arriving in boats with chords of white flags strung from one end to the other, and also on the bank, where they were alighting, were strings of small white flags attached to poles from tree to tree.

Shadipur, where the Sind river and also the

Tulamul flow into the Jhelum, is a very pretty spot with large shady trees and well worth stopping at for those with more leisure, as some pleasant trips can be made from there.

Just beyond, on the right bank, is Naran Bagh with some ruins, and further on, on the same bank and nearer Sumbal, is another, Kara Bagh, with a rather pretty village on a small hill just behind it. Just beyond Sumbal, one the left bank after passing through the bridge, is a bagh which would be a good place to stop at to see Manasbal Lake and also for fishing.

At Sumbal I landed and sent the boat round to await me at Asham at the head of a canal. I had wanted to follow the Jhelum to the Wular Lake and to cross the bottom end of that to Sopor, but my boatman was afraid for the winds on Wular Lake are very sudden and very violent, and woe betide the unfortunate houseboat caught by one in the open; hence I wandered by canals, swamps and backwaters to the very bottom of the lake close to where the Jhelum again emerges from it.

We then walked across the fields past two pretty villages and tried to find the ruins of Anderkut; this we had some difficulty in doing as none of the villagers appeared to know of any. Finally we came across two large piles of stone some distance apart, but too much destroyed and covered to be of interest as they were. In one pile we were shown one stone rather well carved. This was all that remained of King Jayapida's capital.

Near these villages, which the flood water from the river had almost made into islands, I noticed several hollows filled with the bones of cattle, and was told that dying and dead cattle were taken to these places and the rest left to nature.

We tried to reach Asham by what on the map was land, but now was a lake on which we could not get a boat, and after a long walk to the cut from the river, we spied our dunga, which contrary to orders, had left Asham and was flying down the strong current of the cut, and we had great difficulty in arresting the boatman's attention and he in stopping the boat. We had a narrow escape of losing the boat as darkness shortly overtook us. As it was we had to tie up to a bank in what was rightly described as a swamp in the map, and only a short distance from Anderkut. Here myriads of mosquitos invaded us and on my complaining to my Boy about the site he had chosen instead of either Asham or the running stream, he coolly said there were no mosquitos, but as even his green face began to swell I thought it unnecessary to argue the point, so extinguishing all lights had a very hasty meal and retired to bed under my fly-proof net.

A glorious morning followed and we were off at 4.30 a.m. Sheets of water all around and pretty little villages under large shady trees on slight mounds or hillocks, with cattle and horses round them and women drawing water from the floods which surrounded them. There were scores of herons fishing and a fair number of eagles with light brown heads and white and black tails.

Our course lay through a canal with willows and other trees on either banks but with the water on both sides beyond them : sometimes the canal disappeared in the waters. This marshy area receives the flood-water of the Jhelum from above Srinagar by way of the Spill Canal already mentioned.

By the village of Shahgund we cleared the canal and entered the Wular Lake : this, though by no means large, being when full about 15 miles at its longest by 8 at its broadest, is the largest lake in India. On the still morning we passed over it the slight haze over the far shore and the lofty mountains all round the lake rising apparently from the water edge and reflected faultlessly in the dark waters, made a very fine and impressive picture.

A little ahead of us was a country dunga in which a small boy and his sister with a splendid plaited head of hair were poling, and wishing to draw near to obtain a photograph I explained my wishes to the boatman, and he and his boys entered into the chase with such zeal, dodging about after the boat as it tried to get out of our way that the children got afraid, retired into the dunga, and their father came out and took their place.

Shortly afterwards we again entered the Jhelum with Sopor a mile or so ahead. It was a fair sized place, with a very substantial bridge and a pretty mosque on the left bank of the river, just beyond it.

Soon a small boat came alongside with two men in it who had a long chat with my boatman, who then told me these expert fishermen would take me for an hour's fishing below the bridge which was famous for fish, and where some enormous fish, mahseer, have been caught and photographed, so big that not being a fisherman I am afraid to give their weight.

After a little persuasion I gave in and was to pay by results, so much for fishing and so much for a catch. I got into their boat, went ashore with the fishermen, got a rod, fresh bait, &c., and started out for the bridge, where were already other fishermen.

We spun with fresh bait, which I am pleased to say was always killed before being impaled, and by twist of the wire passed through the fish, the dead bait seemed to acquire the movement of a live fish in the water.

The fishermen did their best and worked hard, and I really felt sorry for them, but had to keep up my reputation of not having had even a bite since I took out my licence. So after something over an hour I got taken over to my dunga and proceeded down stream to reach Baramula by night.

Not far below Sopor we passed an enormous timber depot, Dubgam, and then by a large dredger at work, which almost blocked the river, and on along by the banks which the dredger had thrown up.

At one small village a houseboat landed containing a wedding party, which was welcomed by groups of children singing, but the crowd which came out of the houseboat reminded me of a conjurer and his hat.

First twenty-four men with countless children, then crowds of women in brilliant colours, and the groom wearing a turban with an aignette on it—then we drifted by.

The river has also its seamy side, for not far beyond that village we passed a dog eating a corpse and later a vulture on a drowned cow.

At 2 o'clock the wind rose and blew very heavily till 8 p.m., and we had to tie up in a narrow creek which ran into the river about two miles from Baramula, and even there the dunga rocked. I left the boat and walked along the bank, through some prosperous looking villages and estate timber yards, to the town which seemed quite a busy place. On the left bank, about the main road, there were large stables for tongas and ponies and, nearer the river, enormous yards for bullocks from bullock-carts. This is the last place at which the river is navigable, for just below the strong wooden bridge, whose centre span opens, the river becomes a torrent. The town has a pretty situation as the hills tower above it, rising almost sheer from the water, and on one of these are the remains of an old Sikh fort.

About 8.30 p.m. the wind having fallen, we slipped down to a site near the Dak bungalow.

Next day was hot and steamy and about noon rained heavily. Here I was joined by my friend, whose leave, like mine, was expiring, and we arranged for a ride to Gulmarg on the morrow. Owing to the late season this year, this popular hot weather resort for Srinagar folk and others from India, had hardly opened. Two ponies were brought for inspection, one was very poor and refused. The owners pretended they had no others, but turned up in the end with a very good one in its place. I only regretted not having refused both the original ponies, as it was palpably a try-on. There was considerable excitement in Baramula as some of the Maharajah's ladies with their numerous retinue arrived in motor cars at the country house on the Jhelum near the Dak bungalow, and the strand of the river before the house was screened off on both sides, very much interfering with one's usual walk to the bridge and town.

My friend had a houseboat and on this wet day it certainly looked cosier than any dunga; also the little platform above to sit out on was very nice when the weather cleared in the evening: still I think the advantages lie with the dunga and at any rate it is a native or local production.

The 8th June was a beautiful day, and at 8 o'clock we started off on our ponies, with the guide and groom on the third, for GULMARG (Mountain of Flowers). At first the mountains were covered in clouds, but cleared with the heat of the day. We rose steadily 1,500 feet over a ridge behind Baramula, covered with deodars, firs and pines, then down a long gradual slope to the Ningal Nala river, which we crossed and, rising a short distance, rested at the village of Kontor for our horses. It was a pretty spot with large shady walnut and chestnut trees, and a spring rising at their feet. From there the rise was mostly very steep, still there were places where one could get quite a good canter. The road was quite a good one, well looked after and the gradient easy, and as a rule a stream of water rushed along by the roadside with little springs falling into it from either side. The mountain was covered with a forest of fine trees, many growing to a great height, firs, pines of many varieties, thujas, taxodium, sycamores, with bushes of may and dwarf beech, and on the highest parts dwarf rhododendrons and kalmias covered the ground and large white clematis climbed in profuse clusters over the bushes.

By 12.15 we reached the crest of the mountains, a distance of 17 miles from Baramula.

From this ridge and even lower down, fine views are obtained over the plain through which the Jhelum wanders, with Lake Wular to the North, Lake Manisbal more to the North-East, and away to the East distant Srinagar, the whole plain surrounded by lofty ranges in which Haramuk (16,900 feet), Mahadev, and on clear days Nungar Parbat with its 26,000 odd feet, eighty miles away to the North, stand out.

As one approached the crest, one met signs of civilisation: pinewood bathing houses along the stream, now a series of cascades and large electrical plants driven by the waterfalls. On passing over the crest one looked down on a steep road lined with shops, most of them branches of Srinagar firms, on to a green basin about two miles by one, through

PLATE XXIV.

On the road to Gulmarg.

Gulmarg. View N.E. from the ridge.

which a stream wandered, entirely surrounded by fir woods with mountains rising still higher behind on the South side. In these fir woods are dotted scores of pretty wooden villas like chalets, commonly spoken of as huts. On the farthest edge of the basin stood a large wooden Hotel, too small to accommodate its many guests, with a large assembly room some way below and connected with it by a covered passage.

The green basin was used for sports of all kinds—tennis, cricket, golf, polo, &c. It was also a veritable Alpine garden, gentians grew in profusion and anemones in places so thick as to make the ground quite white.

In this delightful spot the European population of Srinagar comes for the two or three hot summer months, as do also numerous visitors.

We had lunch at the Hotel and, after a short rest on the verandah admiring the scene, left at 2.30, arriving back in about four hours.

For anyone wishing to stop at the Hotel it would be advisable to wire or write for rooms as far ahead as possible to avoid disappointment.

On our way I noticed several cases of goître among the villagers, possibly caused by drinking snow water, as some people account for that malady in the Alps.

That night before turning in I settled up with my people. They all scored heavily as they were engaged and paid for a month and had only been with me three weeks; still, with the exception of my Boy, all had been honest and most willing to do anything or go anywhere at any time that I wanted.

With the Boy it was different ; he was a liar and a thief, and it was only because of his knowledge of the country, his fluent English and knowledge of Hindustani, as well as his own language, that I had kept him so long. So when he asked me to write him a testimonial, as was the custom for all servants, I refused, and on his presenting to me his accounts showing money received and paid which, on his showing, left me Rs. 80 in his debt, I easily proved even to his satisfaction—hardly satisfaction—but at any rate incontrovertibly, that he really owed me Rs. 15, and also how he had robbed me over food, oil, &c., how he had altered the figures of a memo I had made of his pay in a notebook of mine, and how absolutely incompetent he was as a valet and servant. As he gave way to tears, probably of disappointment, I finally wrote a testimonial confining myself to the statement that I found him a good guide and useful in getting about.

His downfall was very pleasing to the rest of my people as I saw next morning, for he had been very domineering.

CHAPTER VI.

ON the 9th I was up at 5 a.m., but just before I left in the tonga at 6 o'clock, the head man of Baramula came round to try and pick up some backsheesh. I had never seen him till then and was certain he had done nothing for me, but my boatman and Boy lied for the benefit of their country and I made him a present.

My tonga was followed by that of my friend and we galloped most of the way, our drivers generally racing.

Usually the passenger sits on the back seat of the tonga, the driver and stableman sitting in front; but as by this arrangement one can get no view and besides gets the bad tobacco smoke or worse from the driver and man, I decided to sit by the driver and for my personal safety was glad I did, for the driver of the first part of the day was very sleepy and drove with very loose reins and three times I woke him by a jab in the ribs when his head had fallen on his breast, and, as the road was downhill for the most part alongside the river and anything from 20 to 40 feet above it, I had to keep a sharp eye on the man and the reins.

We had a beautiful ride and no dust, but a haze spoilt the distant view. Our road lay all the way on the left bank and when about ten miles out we passed two ruined temples of much the same design as those already noticed: the second one had been "restored" and spoilt. Fifteen miles or so further, on the right bank and sloping down towards the river and in a lovely position, were the ruins of a bagh and summer residence.

The journey is performed on the stage system, changing one's horses or rather ponies every five or six miles, when the stableman walks them back to the place they started from.

Owing probably to the great demand after the first four or five changes the system this day broke down, and on arriving at a stage we sometimes found that the horses had not arrived back, and then we had to wait or sometimes were told there were none, so went on with the same horses hoping to pick up some on the road or at the next stage. Several times drivers of tongas coming up stopped mine and were going to take away my fairly fresh horses and leave me their tired ones. Needles to say that did not take place with my tonga though it was apparently a recognized custom.

At Chinari, a busy little place with shops along the main road and the usual heavy sleepy-eyed white oxen awaiting by the roadside their turn to move on, we stopped for lunch at the Dak Bungalow.

Then on to Ghari, which we reached at 4 o'clock, where my sleepy driver left after demanding backsheesh, and a very old man came on in his place. He was very torpid, and as my friend's tonga was away out of sight in the distance and words were powerless to urge him on, I regret to say I had to

PLATE XXV.

Posting Station.

Cashmere Goats.

adopt more strenuous methods, after which we raced and at one place a couple of hours later I had even to hold him in. By 6 o'clock we arrived at Domel.

From just below Baramula the river had been a boiling torrent carrying down thousands of cedar (deodar) logs, and just below Ghari it rushed between cliffs about 50 feet high made of conglomerate of enormous boulders.

From Chakoti and right up to Murree, except in the larger villages on the road, the houses were square, squat, one-storey buildings with flat mud overhanging roofs, supported in front by columns or poles forming a sort of verandah. On these roofs one often saw charpoys, or animals feeding. Though Domel bungalow looked very tempting we decided to push on to Dulai, another 9½ miles, so as to reach Murree next day in time to get down to Rawul Pindi the same day if necessary.

Dulai is a pretty spot and the Dak bungalow lies surrounded by trees below the level of the road and just above the river, and though steamy the rooms were good, as was also the service. There was also a Khansamah at this bungalow, as there was in in most of these, so one had one care the less.

Some friends who had left Srinagar this morning in a motor passed us early on the road, but broke down and reached Dulai after us, and worse befell them next day, for halfway up to Murree their car again broke down and they had to send back a long way to telegraph for another car to take them on. So again the tortoise won the race.

The 10th saw us up at 5.30 a.m. ; and after trying to placate the insatiable appetite of Cashmiris for backsheesh we left this charming spot at 6.30 a.m. and, after a grand drive of 12 miles, reached Kohala by 8 o'clock. After a short wait on the border town, while they provided us with strong sturdy ponies far better than we had had so far, we started our upward climb of near 5,000 feet in 29½ miles, which we did at a good trot the whole way, except, of course, at the stages where the horses were changed and which were never found wanting, and arrived at 1 p.m. at our destination.

The haze again obscured our distant views, but the mountain sides were extensively cultivated, and the the series of terraces of paddy or other grain, or vegetables, with a few trees and an odd cottage, right down to the Jhelum, which gradually became more distant and threadlike, made a very pretty picture.

Oleanders, pink and deep rose, were in full bloom and in great profusion about our road, and large herds of fine camels were browsing on the slopes of the mountain.

Murree was packed full, so we had to proceed to Pindi and to leave at 3 o'clock and were lucky to get seats in any car so great was the crowd.

Our car scorched down and there was an unpleasant hot wind and clouds of dust, so we saw little or nothing of this beautiful ride.

At Rawul Pindi we got good and comfortable accommodation at Flashman's Hotel and regretted our trip to Cashmere had ended.

CUSTOMS AND COSTUMES.

THE general costume of men and women of the poorer class is a sort of kimono but closed up the front and with a hole to put the head through, lined, with large cuffs turned back, and also a large collar. If the body of the garment is coloured the cuffs and collars are white, but if the body is white or grey then the cuffs are usually coloured.

The country people usually carry a length of home-made cloth, called puttoo, round them, as a Scotsman would his plaid, which serves them against the cold or rain and acts as a covering at night.

An ordinary piece would cost a few rupees, but ridiculous prices were being asked this year, the reason given being that so many had been sent as blankets to the troops in Mesopotamia !

The well-to-do people use pieces which are well made and of very fine material.

Cashmere has for a very long time been famous for its shawls, and about the end of the Seventeenth Century Bernier wrote: " But what may be considered peculiar and the staple commodity, that which particularly promotes the trade of the country and fills it with wealth, is the prodigious quantity of shawls which they manufacture and which gives occupation even to children."

This industry has very much fallen off but fine shawls are still made, very many from the soft short under-wool of the long-haired Cashmere or rather Thibet goats. This material is called pashmina.

The women of the richer classes wear particularly brilliant coloured tunics and trousers under their grey or dull coloured mantles and their children also wear bright colours. The better class Mahommedan women usually cover the faces or rather their mouths when men are about but the working classes do not.

The little girls of 6—9 are very pretty but their beauty must soon go, for though the women are mostly pleasant-looking, very few indeed can be called pretty. The little children wear bright-coloured tight-fitting caps, heavily ornamented with showy "jewels" and with very heavy flat triangular ornaments hanging at either side of their head with short chains of beads or pearls attached to them: they also wear heavy necklaces and anklets. The women wear long ear-rings with a great number of objects dangling from them which rather resemble a well-filled key-ring.

The little girls have their hair done in rather a peculiar manner: numerous little plaits lengthened by the addition of some foreign black material are joined behind the neck to the two outside plaits which meet in a knot with a tassel or cord hanging from it.

A local Mohammedan told me that girls marry from the age of 12 to 17 and a contract is made by the respective parents of the couple without the interested parties having necessarily met or even seen each other.

The men wear a tight-fitting skull cap, often worked in bright colours, and round it usually wind their turban. The older men stain their white beards red with henna to make themselves look younger.

Henna seems to be in great favour in the East, for besides dyeing finger nails, &c., one often sees white horses or mules with large patches of red on them. One white horse I saw partly coloured blue.

One very common domestic scene, morning and evening, which appealed to me was rice-hulling, usually performed by women and girls. The rice to be hulled was put into a kind of strong wooden bowl, made of a partly hollowed log stood on end and the pounders or pestles were heavy cylindrical pieces of wood about 4 feet by 4 or 5 inches, narrowed at the middle for a hand grip. As a rule two people pounded at a time, striking alternately and standing on opposite sides of the bowl.

The local method of digging, removing gravel or soil from off a road, &c., is certainly original. There are two men to each spade; one, as usual, at the handle, and the other pulling at a rope attached to the haft, just above the spade head. No. 1 inserts the spade in the heap, No. 2 pulls on the rope, lifting a spadeful of earth, which the two proceed to carry to the required spot.

MEMOS.

When telegraphing or writing to anyone in Srinagar or giving an address there, always add Cashmere, as there are other Srinagars in India.

Warm clothing as well as light should be taken for any season of the year, as upon the mountains it is cold, especially at night.

There are good chemists at Srinagar, and possibly at Gulmarg, but elsewhere there are none, so it is advisable to carry a fair supply of the most useful drugs such as quinine.

Very good ordnance maps can be obtained at Srinagar, on the scale of 1 mile to the inch.

INDEX.

L

M.

N

P

R

S

T

U

V

W

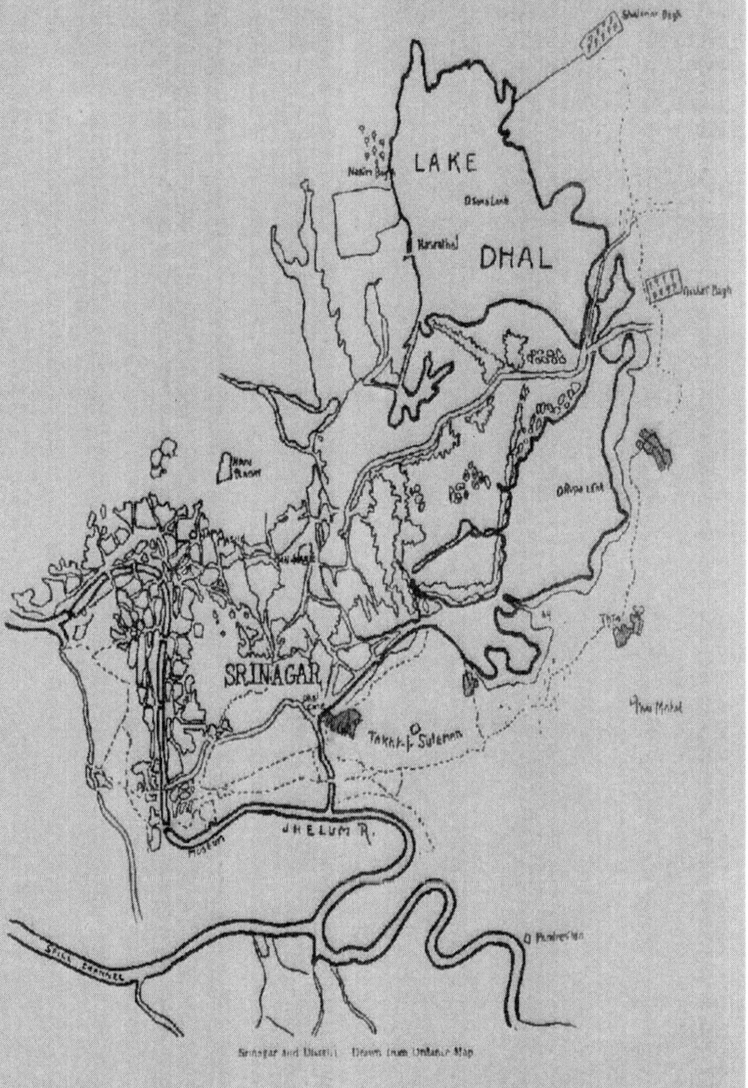

Srinagar and District   Drawn from Ordnance Map

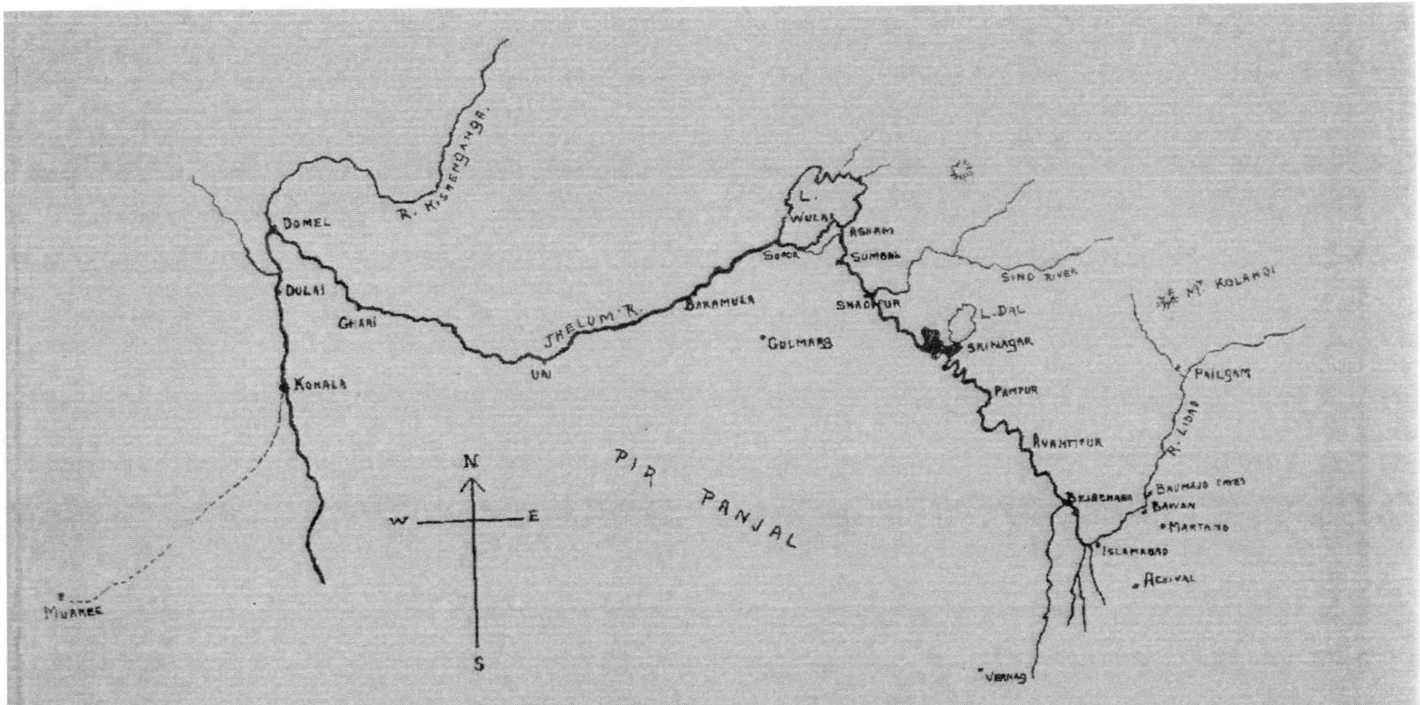

Cashmere Illustrating Journeys.